CALUMET CITY PUBLIC LIBRARY

3 1613 00287 6871

Y0-BYZ-089

Stonewall Jackson

Confederate General

Colonial Leaders

Lord Baltimore
English Politician and Colonist

Benjamin Banneker
American Mathematician and Astronomer

Sir William Berkeley
Governor of Virginia

William Bradford
Governor of Plymouth Colony

Jonathan Edwards
Colonial Religious Leader

Benjamin Franklin
American Statesman, Scientist, and Writer

Anne Hutchinson
Religious Leader

Cotton Mather
Author, Clergyman, and Scholar

Increase Mather
Clergyman and Scholar

James Oglethorpe
Humanitarian and Soldier

William Penn
Founder of Democracy

Sir Walter Raleigh
English Explorer and Author

Caesar Rodney
American Patriot

John Smith
English Explorer and Colonist

Miles Standish
Plymouth Colony Leader

Peter Stuyvesant
Dutch Military Leader

George Whitefield
Clergyman and Scholar

Roger Williams
Founder of Rhode Island

John Winthrop
Politician and Statesman

John Peter Zenger
Free Press Advocate

Revolutionary War Leaders

John Adams
Second U.S. President

Ethan Allen
Revolutionary Hero

Benedict Arnold
Traitor to the Cause

King George III
English Monarch

Nathanael Greene
Military Leader

Nathan Hale
Revolutionary Hero

Alexander Hamilton
First U.S. Secretary of the Treasury

John Hancock
President of the Continental Congress

Patrick Henry
American Statesman and Speaker

John Jay
First Chief Justice of the Supreme Court

Thomas Jefferson
Author of the Declaration of Independence

John Paul Jones
Father of the U.S. Navy

Lafayette
French Freedom Fighter

James Madison
Father of the Constitution

Francis Marion
The Swamp Fox

James Monroe
American Statesman

Thomas Paine
Political Writer

Paul Revere
American Patriot

Betsy Ross
American Patriot

George Washington
First U.S. President

Famous Figures of the Civil War Era

Jefferson Davis
Confederate President

Frederick Douglass
Abolitionist and Author

Ulysses S. Grant
Military Leader and President

Stonewall Jackson
Confederate General

Robert E. Lee
Confederate General

Abraham Lincoln
Civil War President

William Sherman
Union General

Harriet Beecher Stowe
Author of Uncle Tom's Cabin

Sojourner Truth
Abolitionist, Suffragist, and Preacher

Harriet Tubman
Leader of the Underground Railroad

Stonewall Jackson

Confederate General

Martha S. Hewson

Arthur M. Schlesinger, jr.
Senior Consulting Editor

Chelsea House Publishers

Philadelphia

CALUMET CITY PUBLIC LIBRARY

The author would like to thank the following people for their help with this book: Don Johnson, park ranger/historian at Manassas National Battlefield Park; Kathy Tauber, librarian at Worcester Elementary School; Deborah Heiligman, Jackie Ziegler, and Craig Ziegler.

Produced by 21st Century Publishing and Communications, Inc. New York, NY. http://www.21cpc.com

CHELSEA HOUSE PUBLISHERS
Production Manager Pamela Loos
Art Director Sara Davis
Director of Photography Judy L. Hasday
Managing Editor James D. Gallagher
Senior Production Editor J. Christopher Higgins

Staff for *STONEWALL JACKSON*
Project Editor Anne Hill
Associate Art Director Takeshi Takahashi
Series Design Keith Trego

©2001 by Chelsea House Publishers, a subsidiary of Haights Cross Communications. All rights reserved. Printed and bound in the United States of America.

The Chelsea House World Wide Web address is http://www.chelseahouse.com

First Printing
1 3 5 7 9 8 6 4 2

Library of Congress Cataloging-in-Publication Data

Hewson, Martha S.
    Stonewall Jackson / by Martha S. Hewson.
       p. cm. — (Famous figures of the Civil War era)
    Includes bibliographical references and index.
    ISBN 0-7910-6002-0 — ISBN 0-7910-6140-X (pbk.)
      1. Jackson, Stonewall, 1824-1863—Juvenile literature. 2. Generals—Confederate States of America—Biography—Juvenile literature. 3. Confederate States of America. Army—Biography—Juvenile literature. 4. United States—History—Civil War, 1861-1865—Campaigns—Juvenile literature. [1. Jackson, Stonewall, 1824-1863. 2. Generals. 3. United States—History—Civil War, 1861-1865.] I. Title. II. Series.

E467.1.J15 H59 2000
973.7'3'092—dc21   00-035866
[B]   CIP

Publisher's Note: In Colonial, Revolutionary War, and Civil War Era America, there were no standard rules for spelling, punctuation, capitalization, or grammar. Some of the quotations that appear in the Colonial Leaders, Revolutionary War Leaders, and Famous Figures of the Civil War Era series come from original documents and letters written during this time in history. Original quotations reflect writing inconsistencies of the period.

Contents

Tom Jackson was born on a winter night in Clarksburg, Virginia. No one in his family would ever have guessed that the new baby would someday become a famous military leader.

From Virginia to West Point

On that cold winter night, everybody agreed on one thing at Jonathan Jackson's house. His wife, Julia, had given birth to a baby boy. But when was he born? The doctor thought the baby had arrived a few minutes before midnight on January 20. The family was sure he was born a few minutes into the new day.

The Jacksons won. January 21, 1824, became the birthday of Thomas Jonathan Jackson. Little did the Jackson family know that one day people all over the world would care about Tom's birthday. He would grow up to become one of the most famous Confederate generals in the American Civil War.

Tom's family lived in a brick house along the main road in Clarksburg. At that time, the town was in Virginia. During the Civil War, that part of the state became West Virginia.

Tom's father was a lawyer. He was also a gambler, who liked to play cards. He often owed people money. Tom had an older sister, Elizabeth, and an older brother, Warren. When Tom was two, Elizabeth came down with typhoid fever. Tom's mother was about to have another baby. She couldn't take care of Elizabeth. So Tom's father took over the nursing duties. By late March, both father and daughter were dead.

Tom was too young to remember those sad times. The day after his father died, he had a new baby sister, Laura. Tom's mother had to sell the house and everything in it to pay her husband's **debts**. She taught school for a while and took in sewing. Still, the family was very poor.

In 1830, Julia married again. By the time Tom was seven, his stepfather was in debt. Julia was pregnant again and was very sick. First she sent Warren away to live with her family. She tried to keep Tom and Laura at home but finally decided to send them to live with the Jackson family.

Tom loved his mother very much. He was terribly upset when his Uncle Cummins came to get him and Laura. Tom's mother gave the children one last hug. She cried and cried. Tom never forgot that awful day. A few months later, Julia called her children back for a final visit. She never recovered from the illness and after giving birth to another child, she died on December 4, 1831.

Many years later, Tom's wife, Anna, said that her husband didn't talk much about his childhood. That's because it was the saddest period of his life.

Jackson's Mill near Weston, Virginia, was the name of the place where Tom went to live. The large property included a farm as well as a sawmill and grain mill. Tom's stepgrandmother lived there along with his six uncles and two aunts. Uncle Cummins was in charge.

Tom's chances for education were limited. When he went to school, it was only for a few months at a time. Laura was not only Tom's little sister but also his best friend. He rowed her across the West Fork River to play under the trees. Together they trapped rabbits and made maple sugar. But four years later, Laura was sent to live with other relatives.

When Tom was 12, his brother, Warren, came for a visit. Warren had a plan. They would visit Laura. Then they'd make some money by selling firewood to passing steamboats on the Ohio River. The boys traveled down the Ohio River until it met the Mississippi River. There they set up their business on an island. When they came home six months later, neither boy would talk about what had happened, but they were very dirty, sick, and tired.

Tom didn't spend much time in school (which probably looked like this one) but realized he needed to go to college to get ahead in life.

As Tom got older, he worked for Cummins on the farm and at the mill. When Cummins wanted to race horses, Tom was the jockey. He was never very graceful in the saddle, but he won the races.

When he was 16, Tom spent a few months teaching school. At 17, he became a **constable**. The job included riding around the county to collect debts. That same year, Warren died. Laura was the only one left from Tom's original family.

In January 1842, Tom turned 18. He knew he needed more education to get somewhere in life. His congressman announced that there was an opening at the U.S. Military Academy at West Point, New York. Tom was interested. This would be a chance to get a good education for free.

Tom was not the only one in town who wanted to be a West Point cadet, however. A boy named Gibson Butcher also applied. In mid-April, Tom got the bad news. Butcher would be the one going to New York. Butcher showed up at West Point on June 3 but left one day later. He knew right away that he would hate the strict, rule-filled life of a cadet.

Tom suddenly had another chance. The whole town of Weston seemed to get behind him. People wrote letters to Congressman Samuel Hays, urging that Tom get the position. A lawyer helped Tom study for the exam he would take once he reached West Point.

But first, Tom had to see Congressman Hays in Washington, which was 250 miles away. He and a slave rode by horse to catch the stagecoach at Clarksburg, Virginia. But they were an hour late. Tom and the slave chased the stagecoach as fast as they could through the rain. After 20 miles they caught up with it and Tom hopped aboard. The slave returned home with Tom's horse. The stagecoach took Tom to Green Valley Depot, 16 miles east of Cumberland, Maryland. There he boarded a Baltimore and Ohio train, and made the final leg of his trip to Washington.

Congressman Hays was surprised to see Tom. He didn't even know that Butcher had left West Point. But Hays was impressed with Tom and the letters he had brought from Weston. Within a day, Tom was on his way again. This time he was headed to West Point, which sat on a cliff above the Hudson River.

Tom arrived at the academy with his saddle-bags slung over his shoulder. He was wearing homespun clothes and a broad-brimmed hat.

This is the view Tom saw from the military academy at West Point. There he learned respect for rules, which brought order to his hectic life.

Another cadet noticed the look on Tom's face. "That fellow looks as if he had come to stay," said the cadet.

Tom may have been there to stay, but it wasn't going to be easy. His first hurdle was the entrance exam. As part of the test, each young man had to do a math problem at the blackboard. When it was his turn, Tom was very nervous. Sweat streamed down his face. As he worked the fractions problem, he wiped his face with the cuffs of his coat. When he finally finished, he was relieved–and so was everyone else in the room. Tom barely passed the exam. When the list of those who passed was posted, his name was last.

West Point cadets were expected to learn how to ride horses, use swords, and handle **artillery**. Over four years, cadets' studies included math, engineering, French, drawing, science, and history. Tom's lack of schooling showed up right away. But he was determined to stay. One classmate remembered Tom studying late into the night by firelight.

Tom kept trying. He passed the exams, and he followed the rules. He also started a notebook of maxims, or rules, for himself. Many of the rules were about improving himself or dealing with other people. Throughout his life, rules would be a comfort to Tom. They gave him an orderly way to deal with the ups and downs of life.

Life at West Point was not easy for the cadets. There were many rules. Every item in a cadet's room had to be put in exactly the right place. His clothing and equipment had to look perfect. He was only allowed to take a bath once a week. If he wanted another one, he had to ask special permission.

Every time a cadet broke a rule, a point called a demerit was marked against him. A cadet was sent home if he received 200 demerits in a year. In Tom's third year, he got no demerits—a remarkable feat.

At West Point, Tom's health began to worry him. He'd had trouble with his stomach for several years. He decided that he must sit perfectly straight. That way his internal organs wouldn't press on each other. He thought that one of his legs was larger than the other. He also sensed that one of his arms was heavier. He would often raise his arm, letting blood flow back to his body. That made his arm feel lighter.

Tom was very quiet. He did make a few friends. But other cadets thought he was odd, and they played jokes on him. It also didn't help that he always followed the rules. Once, when the cadets were marching, it started raining heavily. The others ran for shelter, but Tom kept on marching.

Tom also kept on studying. Throughout the four years, Tom's class rank rose steadily. When he graduated in 1846, he was 17th out of 59 of his classmates. Other cadets said that if there had been a fifth year, "Old Jack," as he was called, would have finished first.

He had proven his favorite maxim: "You may be whatever you resolve to be."

This portrait shows Tom as a young man in uniform.
By the time he was 27, Tom had fought in the Mexican
War and become a teacher at Virginia Military Institute.

2

Taking Up Teaching

Tom and the West Point class of 1846 marched off to the Mexican War. The United States had declared war on Mexico in May 1846. Tom was assigned to the artillery. He was eager to get into battle and make a name for himself.

Tom reached Texas in September, only to find that the fighting had stopped. An eight-week **truce** had just been called. Delay followed delay. Tom grew impatient. He told one officer, "I really envy you men who have been in action."

Finally, six months later, Tom saw his first action at Veracruz. Something came over him in battle.

Suddenly he was calm and in control. He noticed it, and so did the other soldiers.

For years, trouble had been brewing between Mexico and the United States. Texas had left Mexico in 1836 and joined the United States in 1845. Mexico still owned California and other land in the Southwest. Mexico's leaders feared that the United States wanted to take over that land, too. They were right.

The two countries disagreed over the location of the border between Texas and Mexico. In May 1846, Mexican soldiers crossed the U.S. border into Texas. The United States had finally found a reason to declare war.

General Winfield Scott was in charge of the American **troops**. The way to win the war was to seize the enemy's capital. Scott set his sights on Mexico City. Along the way, Tom fought in the battles of Cerro Gordo, Contreras, and Churubusco.

At last, only one thing stood between Scott's army and Mexico City—an enormous castle at Chapultepec. Tom started down the road to the castle with his men and two pieces of artillery. Six horses pulled each gun. Suddenly the Mexicans began firing down from the castle. All of the horses were either killed or wounded. Tom's men

Tom fought in many battles in the Mexican War (like the one shown here). He was promoted because of his bravery.

ran for cover. With horses and men gone, there was no way to move the big guns.

But Tom stayed calm. He walked back and forth along the road, shouting to his men, "There is no danger! See? I am not hit!" He would later say that this was the only lie he ever told.

With the help of another man, Tom dragged a big gun into place and started firing. He suddenly became a war hero. On September 14, 1847, the Americans entered Mexico City.

Years later, Tom was asked two questions about those last days of the Mexican War. Did he ever think of running away at Chapultepec? Did it bother him that his guns had killed civilians fleeing Mexico City? His answer to both questions was basically the same: "My duty is to obey orders!" Tom had done that and more. At the end of the war, he was promoted to the rank of first lieutenant.

The war was over, but the American army stayed in Mexico City until July 1848. Tom had time to get to know the city and its people. He liked almost everything about Mexico—the Spanish language, the weather, as well as the tropical fruits and flowers. He was invited into many homes. He also studied Spanish and religion. During his stay in Mexico City, Tom prayed and read his Bible every day. He was fascinated by the Catholic churches in Mexico.

Then he returned to the United States. For the

next two years, he was assigned to Fort Hamilton, near New York City. Without a war to think about, Tom focused on his health. His stomach was hurting again. His arm was heavy. Bright light bothered his eyes. He went from doctor to doctor and found some relief with **hydropathy**. A simple diet also seemed to help. He liked plain meat, stale bread, and water. If he was invited to someone's house for dinner, he brought along his own food. Tom wondered if his illnesses were God's punishment for his sins. He didn't know if he had been **baptized**. So he was baptized on April 29, 1849.

Tom was next assigned to Fort Meade in Florida. He spent only five months there. The work was boring, and he fought with his commanding officer. There was little hope of promotion. So he felt it was time to leave the army. When he was offered a teaching job at Virginia Military Institute (VMI) in Lexington, Virginia, he accepted happily. VMI had modeled itself after West Point.

For the next 10 years, Tom was a professor of

natural and experimental philosophy. He was also an artillery instructor. Natural philosophy included the study of sound, light, and the stars. Today these subjects are part of physics. Natural philosophy was not an easy subject, and Tom couldn't really help his students. At first, he was still learning the subject himself. But the main problem was that he didn't have a gift for teaching. In 1856, some former students tried to have him removed. They didn't succeed.

His students played pranks on Major Jackson, as he was called at VMI. They made fun of him and gave him nicknames. To many cadets, Tom seemed humorless and boring. But some in the town realized he was a good person. One person who appreciated him was a woman named Elinor "Ellie" Junkin. Tom got to know Ellie and married her on August 4, 1853. She was soon expecting a baby. Finally, at the age of 30, Tom was going to have a family of his own.

On October 22, 1854, Ellie delivered a baby boy. But something went terribly wrong. The

A statue of Tom stands at an entrance to VMI, where he taught as a young man. The buildings at VMI were modeled after those at West Point.

child was born dead. Later that same day, Ellie also died. The world fell in on Tom. For a long time afterward, he visited Ellie's grave every day.

In 1856, Tom spent the summer in Europe. After returning home, he decided he was ready to love again. Tom already had someone in mind. He had met Mary Anna Morrison when she was visiting relatives in Lexington. But he had been engaged to Ellie at the time. Mary Anna Morrison was the daughter of a **pastor** in the Presbyterian Church. Tom started to write to Anna, as she was known. At Christmastime, he went to visit her at her home in North Carolina. They were married on July 16, 1857.

Like many other people, Anna was impressed with her new husband's honesty. Soon after their wedding, they were taking a walk. Anna spied some apples that had fallen from a tree. She asked him to pick them up for a snack. But Tom said, "No, I do not think it would be right to do that." He would not take them without the owner's permission.

On April 30, 1858, Anna gave birth to a girl. She was named Mary Graham, after Anna's mother. But within a few weeks, the baby died. The Jacksons were crushed. Tom found some comfort in religion. He felt that it was their duty to obey God and not question what had happened.

Tom had joined the Presbyterian Church seven

years earlier. He was a **deacon** and had started a Sunday school for African Americans, both free and slave. He gave one-tenth of his pay to the church. He'd continue to do that while fighting in the Civil War.

Prayer filled his life. He prayed whenever he took a sip of water or opened a letter. He prayed while waiting for his students to file into and out of class. Tom could pray by himself or in front of his family. But when his pastor asked him to lead prayers at church, he had trouble. Tom felt terrible. His pastor was like his commanding officer. He had a duty to lead those prayers, so Tom practiced until he could do it easily.

In November 1858, Tom bought an old brick house in Lexington. It needed a lot of work, but Tom didn't mind. He liked working around the house, fixing things up for Anna. He also enjoyed working in his garden. In time, he bought 18 acres for a farm, growing wheat and vegetables.

Every morning, he woke up at 6 A.M. and

In this portrait, Tom appears with his second wife, Anna, and their daughter Julia. He loved working in the garden and being with his family.

prayed. Then he took a cold bath, followed by a brisk walk. At 7 A.M., he led family prayers. After breakfast, he spent three hours teaching at VMI. Near the end of the school term, he spent an hour each afternoon at artillery drill.

After teaching, he returned home. He stood at a tall desk for two hours and studied his Bible and textbooks. At 1 P.M., he ate lunch. He often spent the afternoon working in his garden. Sometimes he would take Anna along when he went to work on the farm.

After supper, he would spend some time relaxing. He didn't think it was good for his health to work right after supper. His eyes were still bothering him, so he didn't like to read at night. Instead, he would review his lessons. He'd tell Anna not to talk to him. Then he'd take his chair and face the wall and go over his lessons in his head.

After finishing reviewing, he was ready to talk to Anna or have her read to him. Sometimes they went for a carriage ride by moonlight. "He was intensely fond of his home," Anna said, "and it was there he found his greatest happiness."

But the Civil War was coming. Tom would soon have to leave home and his happy life with Anna.

The Confederate army's attack on Fort Sumter, South Carolina, (shown here) marked the beginning of the Civil War. Tom had to leave his family and take charge of Virginia's troops.

3

Beginning of the War

When the Civil War began, Tom owned six slaves. He thought the Bible said that slavery was acceptable. However other people in the country were questioning slavery. Most of them lived in the North. Some felt settlers should not have slaves in the newly settled Western lands. Others argued that slavery should not exist at all.

In Lexington, there was talk of war for much of 1860. Tom trusted that God would take care of everything. He continued to teach his classes and enjoy his life with Anna. He also continued to worry about his health. By this time, he had trouble with his hearing.

3 1613 00287 6871

CALUMET CITY PUBLIC LIBRARY

In November 1860, Abraham Lincoln was elected president. Southerners were upset. They feared the president would do away with slavery. On December 20, South Carolina became the first state to **secede**. By February 1861, seven states had left the Union. They formed the Confederate States of America.

Many of the VMI cadets couldn't wait to get into war, but not Tom. He had seen the horrors of battle in Mexico. He also didn't want Virginia to secede. Anna said that Tom thought "it was better for the South to fight for her rights *in the Union than out of it*." Tom wouldn't fight just to save slavery. But if Virginia seceded or was attacked, he would go with his state.

In April 1861, a series of

A former preacher, John Brown believed that slavery should be done away with completely. In October 1859, he seized the arsenal at Harpers Ferry and planned to lead a slave revolt. But he was captured before he could succeed. He was sentenced to die. In December 1859, Tom went to the hanging with a group of VMI cadets. Their job was to keep anyone from trying to rescue Brown.

events led to war. On April 12, the Confederates attacked Fort Sumter in Charleston Harbor, South Carolina. That event led President Lincoln to ask the states for 75,000 **volunteer** soldiers. For the South, this meant war. Four more states, including Virginia, left the Union.

In those last days of April, Tom knew he would be leaving home. He hoped the orders wouldn't come on Sunday. That was God's day and he didn't like to travel on Sundays. But nevertheless, early on Sunday morning, April 21, there was a knock on his door. His orders had arrived. He was instructed to take some VMI cadets to Richmond.

Tom did not wait for breakfast that morning. He hurried over to VMI to get ready. At 11 A.M., he came home and ate a quick breakfast. Then he read the Bible and prayed with Anna. He kissed her good-bye and rode back to VMI.

Tom's pastor prayed for the cadets. Everyone was ready to go. But Tom's orders were to leave at 12:30, which was still a few minutes away.

During the Civil War, trains were used to transport army forces and supplies. Here, Union troops at a train station set off to war.

Tom always followed orders. He pulled out a stool and sat down. Everyone waited. Finally a clock chimed the half hour. Tom climbed on his horse and gave the command to move out.

Tom was riding off to war on a Sunday. In his mind, he was doing God's work. Tom thought that if God hadn't wanted the war, He wouldn't have allowed it to begin.

Tom delivered the cadets to Richmond. He was made a colonel and sent north to Harpers Ferry, Virginia. The Confederates had seized the **arsenal**. The Union troops had fled.

Tom's job was to take charge of Virginia's troops. All kinds of men had volunteered to be soldiers–farmers, clerks, and gentlemen. They were excited about fighting in a real war but didn't know much about being soldiers. Still, they had a good time in camp until Tom arrived.

Tom was back at war, and he knew what to do. He brought order to the camp and put artillery in place to defend the town.

Many more troops poured into Harpers Ferry. General Joseph E. Johnston arrived to take over. Tom was then put in charge of the First Virginia Brigade. Johnston believed that Harpers

Ferry was much too difficult to defend and so he decided to move the troops to Winchester, Virginia, not too far away.

On July 2, 1861, Tom and his men saw their first action. It was just a minor battle at Falling Waters. But Tom helped his men stay calm, even when they had to **retreat**. He was soon promoted to brigadier general.

Meanwhile President Lincoln wanted more action, urging the Union army to march directly on to Richmond, Virginia, the South's capital. On July 16, 1861, Union General Irvin McDowell marched out of Washington accompanied by 35,000 troops. He was

The Civil War is sometimes called "The Brothers' War." Some families had soldiers in both the Union and Confederate armies. The war also divided Tom's family, classmates, and friends. Tom's sister, Laura, supported the Union. Brother and sister stopped writing to each other once the war began.

Friends were also divided. One-third of the graduates of Tom's class at West Point became generals in the war. Ten fought for the South, while twelve fought for the North. Joe Lightburn was a friend from Tom's teenage years. Tom became a Confederate general, and Joe was a Union general.

heading south for Manassas, Virginia. Manassas was a very important transportation center. Two railroads met at that point and armies needed railroads to move troops and supplies.

However, waiting at Manassas was Southern general P.G.T. Beauregard. He had 22,000 troops but knew he needed more men right away. He asked General Johnston for immediate assistance, and Johnston sent 10,000 more men. Tom's brigade led the troops out of Winchester. They made part of the trip by rail. This was one of the first times that trains were used to move troops to battles.

The First Battle of Manassas was fought on a hot, humid day. Union troops fired the first shot at about 6 A.M. on Sunday, July 21. The two armies fought hard throughout the morning. The average age of the soldiers was 19 years old, and they had never been in a war. They had no idea what to expect or what to do. Both sides had made complete battle plans. But it was almost impossible to carry them out with untrained men.

It was also very hard to tell who the enemy was. At the time, both the Union and Confederate flags looked very much alike. Northern soldiers were not wearing blue uniforms yet. And Southern soldiers weren't wearing gray yet either. In fact, there were more than 200 different kinds of uniforms being worn on the field of battle that day. Tom was wearing his blue VMI uniform.

For a while, it seemed that the Union might win. Confederate soldiers began retreating. But Tom stayed calm. He didn't charge ahead into the battle. He looked around and found a good place to put his men and artillery. For more than two hours, Tom kept his men in place. Enemy shells exploded over their heads. The noise was frightening. Tom rode back and forth, talking calmly to his men. He didn't panic, even when he was wounded in the hand.

Confederate general Barnard Bee rode his horse into the woods behind Tom's line. He was

At the beginning of the war, soldiers wore many different kinds of uniforms. Here, charging troops wear VMI uniforms.

looking for his own troops. He found some of them, but they had no officers to lead them back into battle. They quickly agreed to follow Bee.

Standing in his stirrups, Bee pointed his sword at Tom. "There stands Jackson like a stone wall," he shouted. He urged his men to go to Tom's assistance.

Troops began to form on either side of Tom's line. When it was time to charge the enemy, Tom told them to "yell like furies!" For the first time, the famous rebel yell was heard in battle.

Soon more Confederate troops arrived on the scene. By the end of the afternoon, they had won the First Battle of Manassas. Northern troops went dashing back to Washington. The Union named this 1861 battle Bull Run, after a stream on the battlefield. This was the first big battle fought in the war. Both sides would later meet again to fight the Second Battle of Manassas, or Bull Run.

Many men were killed in the first battle. One of them was General Bee. He never knew that he had given Tom his famous nickname. Within three days, a Richmond newspaper picked up the story of "Stonewall" Jackson and his brigade. They were on their way to becoming famous.

But Tom didn't take credit for the victory. He wrote to Anna, saying that he felt that honor belonged to God. The battle had been fought on her birthday. He joked that he would never have an excuse for forgetting Anna's birthday.

Tom rests at his tent between battles. In the Valley campaign, Tom's troops successfully protected an area needed to provide food for the Confederate army.

Saving the Valley

The First Battle of Manassas was a shock to both North and South. Both sides recognized they weren't really prepared for war. They needed to train their troops and get organized. Tom worked on making his men better soldiers. His wounded hand hurt. But overall, his health had improved.

Tom was promoted to major general in October 1861 and put in charge of the Shenandoah Valley District. The Shenandoah Valley lay between two mountain ranges in Virginia. But his promotion also came with bad news. He could not take his brigade with him. Tom was upset and so were his men.

They liked their commander.

Tom was different from other officers. He didn't drink, smoke, or gamble. He always made his men follow the rules, but they liked him anyway because he treated them well. If they had to move something heavy, the general got off his horse to help. He tried to make sure his soldiers had enough to eat.

Tom's men were happy when the orders were changed. They could now go with their general. Tom settled into Winchester, the main town in the northern part of the valley. He sent for Anna, who arrived in mid-November.

As winter came, Tom worried about Union forces at Romney. He thought his men should attack immediately. If they waited until spring, the Union would have a chance to build up its troops. On January 1, 1862, Tom and his men headed for Romney. By the time they got there, the Union troops had fled.

The Jacksons had moved in with a Presbyterian pastor's family. When Tom wasn't busy with army affairs, he played with the children in the house. Every morning, he gave one of the little boys a piggyback ride downstairs to breakfast. But the quiet days in Winchester couldn't last forever. By March, Tom thought Anna should move further south. Anna was expecting a baby when she left.

Tom withdrew his troops from Winchester. The Union immediately seized the town. Tom didn't want to abandon Winchester, but he had other work to do.

A new general was in charge of the Union troops. General George McClellan had been in Tom's class at West Point. He had a different idea for attacking Richmond. He wasn't going to march his troops down from Washington. Instead, he was planning to take them by water to the area between the York River and James River. Then he would march north to Richmond. Other Union troops would join him there, and they would seize the Confederate capital.

On Sunday, March 23, Tom's men attacked

Union troops at Kernstown. Tom didn't like fighting on Sunday, but he didn't dare wait another day. When the battle was over, it didn't seem like a victory for Tom. There had been too many Union soldiers, and Tom's men were forced to retreat.

But Tom had really scared Lincoln and some of the Union generals. Union troops had been planning to march from Washington to join McClellan at Richmond. After the Kernstown attack, however, Lincoln feared that the Confederates might attack Washington. He wanted more troops left behind to guard the city.

Tom forced the Union

In March 1862, Tom asked a skilled mapmaker, Jedediah Hotchkiss, to make a map of the valley for him. The general wanted more than a simple map. He wanted Hotchkiss to mark all the places where an army might launch an attack or set up a solid defense. He would soon be starting his campaign in the Shenandoah Valley.

Lack of good maps was a problem in the early years of the war, especially for the South. Military schools were the only places that taught mapmaking. Hotchkiss, however, had taught himself the skills he needed.

This portrait shows Union general George McClellan. He and Tom had been classmates at West Point but found themselves on opposing sides during the Civil War.

army to focus on the Shenandoah Valley. The valley covered more than 150 miles from north to south. It was a huge area to protect, and Tom did not have many men.

The valley was an important source of food for the Confederate army. Tom also knew he had to tie up the Union troops in the valley, so they couldn't join McClellan. His Valley campaign depended on surprise, speed, and secrecy. It has been called one of the great **military campaigns** of history.

By late April, the Union generals thought Tom had left the valley. Even his own men thought they were leaving. But on May 8, Tom suddenly reversed direction and struck Union forces near McDowell, Virginia. Then he pushed on to Front Royal and defeated Union general Nathaniel Banks there on May 23. Two days later, he fought Banks again at Winchester. Tom finally drove Banks and his army across the Potomac River and into Maryland.

Once again, Winchester belonged to the Confederates. Tom was a hero as he rode through the town. "The people seemed nearly frantic with joy," he wrote to Anna. "Our entrance into Winchester was one of the most

Tom makes a triumphant entrance into Winchester, Virginia, after recapturing the town. He was proud to be greeted as a hero on that day.

stirring scenes of my life."

But Tom did not have time to enjoy his great victory. He headed south in the valley. Two Union armies set out to catch him. Their plan was to trap Tom's army between them and completely crush it. But Tom was too quick for them. On June 8, he defeated one Union army at Cross Keys. The next day, he took on the other one at Port Republic. He managed to defeat both armies before they could unite and catch him.

The Valley campaign was over, and Tom was the winner. In 40 days, he had marched his men more than 400 miles. At times, they traveled so quickly that they were compared to soldiers on horseback. They were called the "foot cavalry."

How had they done it? Some days they had marched more than 35 miles. When their supply wagons couldn't keep up, they didn't eat. Jackson believed in getting a very early start. He made his men get up at 3 A.M. He kept all of them going by ordering 10-minute rest periods every hour. Everyone was expected to lie down to rest–even his horse, Little Sorrel.

Tom had lost about 3,000 men in battles.

The Union's losses were twice as high. Tom's men had fought six major battles and a dozen minor ones. They had captured tons of food, weapons, and medical supplies. They had taken on armies three times their own size. Perhaps most important, they had kept 40,000 Union soldiers from helping McClellan.

Tom's success came at a time when the South needed a victory. His fame spread overseas. When he later captured some Union soldiers, they bragged that they'd had the honor of being captured by Stonewall Jackson.

Confederate General Robert E. Lee was in command of the Army of Northern Virginia. He needed Tom's help to drive McClellan away from Richmond. The Seven Days campaign was about to begin.

Adding Tom's troops, Lee would have 80,000 men. Lee planned to trick McClellan, who had 100,000 men. Lee planned to have some men stay in front of McClellan's troops. While McClellan focused on them, Tom and three other generals would hit McClellan from other directions.

But Tom was late. He missed the Battle of Mechanicsville on June 26. The next day, he took the wrong road and ended up two hours late for the Battle of Gaines' Mill. The Confederates kept after McClellan, who thought the enemy had more men than they really did. The Union began a retreat toward the James River. Lee fought every step of the way.

On June 30, the two sides clashed at Frayser's Farm. Tom was nearby, but he didn't jump into the battle. He was usually so eager to fight. Why was he acting so strangely during the Seven Days battles? That question has puzzled historians. They have offered many explanations: Jackson was ill at the time. He was exhausted from the Valley campaign. He was in an unfamiliar part of the state. In the valley, he was in charge. Here, he had to take orders. And either he didn't have orders, or he didn't understand them.

On July 1, Tom showed up on time for the Battle of Malvern Hill. He seemed more like himself this time. When an officer complained that he couldn't do what Tom ordered, Tom told him to obey anyway.

During the Seven Days campaign, Lee's army had 20,000 **casualties**. He lost one quarter of his men. Yet he succeeded in driving away McClellan.

General Robert E. Lee (left) confers with Tom. Lee thought of Tom as a good friend as well as one of his best officers.

On to Maryland

As McClellan began retreating, Tom wanted to go after him. But by the time he could get anyone to agree, McClellan had escaped.

Stonewall was a tough general. He had a cold, hard side. If soldiers from his own army **deserted**, he believed they should be shot. Those who refused to keep up with the line of march should also be punished. But he also had a very gentle side. He loved children, and he loved Anna. His letters to her were cheerful and full of love. He wrote of things that they would do together when the war was over.

Some Southern officers felt that Tom had let them

down during the Seven Days campaign. If General Lee was disappointed in Tom, he never said anything. In the summer of 1862, Lee gave Tom a new assignment: to strike at Union general John Pope.

Tom first tangled with some of Pope's forces at Cedar Mountain on August 9. For much of the battle, the North had the upper hand. But at a critical point, Tom rode in among his men. Waving his sword, he urged them on. The Confederates beat back the Northern soldiers.

Meanwhile, McClellan was shipping his troops north. He was certain he needed 100,000 more troops to take Richmond. Lincoln offered him only 50,000. McClellan said no. But Lincoln ordered him north anyway.

In May 1861, Tom's men captured some Union trains with horses on board. Tom bought two of them. The small brown horse soon became his favorite. He rode Little Sorrel in all his battles. He compared riding the horse to rocking in a cradle. In fact, Tom sometimes fell asleep in the saddle.

Little Sorrel could keep going all day, and that's what Tom needed. After Little Sorrel died at age 36, his hide was mounted. The horse can still be seen today at the Virginia Military Institute Museum.

Lee also ordered Tom to head north. Lee wanted to keep Pope's army from joining McClellan's men. Tom marched his men more than 50 miles in two days. His goal was to get behind Pope and destroy a railroad. Tom's troops were marching among the enemy and he didn't want the enemy to hear them. Secrecy was important to Tom's plans. But Tom's officers often felt that he kept too much information to himself. What if he was killed? No one would know what to do.

But that wasn't a problem at the moment. They were fooling the enemy. Pope thought Tom's men were marching back to the Shenandoah Valley.

On August 26, Tom's men caused a big train wreck. The wreck tied up the railroad. Pope recognized that Tom wasn't in the Shenandoah Valley. In fact, he was back near Manassas, Virginia. That was where he and his brigade had earned the Stonewall nickname the year before.

Manassas Junction was also the site of a huge Union supply depot. On August 27, Tom's men drove out the Union troops and helped themselves to the supplies. Tom's troops were ragged and hungry. Many had been marching barefoot. Suddenly they found everything they could want. "For my part," wrote one soldier, "I got a toothbrush, a box of candles, a quantity of lobster salad, a barrel of coffee, and other things." When they were done feasting, the soldiers took what they could carry, then burned the rest.

Pope was furious. On the evening of August 28, the two armies exchanged fire. By the next morning, Tom's men were well hidden. In the 1850s, a railroad bed had been dug, but no track was ever laid. Tom's men lay hidden down in the railroad bed.

Pope launched attack after attack. By the end of the next day, he was sure that he could beat Tom. He did not realize that Tom was no longer alone. General James Longstreet had arrived with fresh Confederate troops. When Pope attacked on August 30, Longstreet drove him back toward Washington. There were more than 24,000 casualties at the Second Battle of Manassas.

After the Confederate victory at the Second Battle of Manassas (shown here), General Lee decided the time was right to invade the North.

Lee decided that the time was right to invade the North. His target was Maryland. He hoped that men from Maryland would join his army. He also hoped to get supplies there.

On Friday, September 5, the Confederate troops waded into the Potomac River. The water was waist-deep. A band led the way. When it reached the Maryland shore, it began to play "Maryland, My Maryland." The people of Maryland swarmed around Lee and Tom. They wanted to see the famous generals. But few men wanted to join their army.

Tom became someone to be feared in the North. No one knew where he would turn up next. Would he strike at Philadelphia? Lee did not send Tom farther north. Instead, Lee took a chance and divided his army. He hoped to get his troops back together again before McClellan could attack. Lee knew that McClellan was always slow to act. He was right. A Union soldier found a copy of Lee's orders and gave them to McClellan. But the Union general still didn't act quickly.

Lee sent Tom to take over Harpers Ferry, which was under the Union's control. Lee needed Harpers Ferry to get supplies from the Shenandoah Valley. On the way to Harpers Ferry, Tom went through Martinsburg, Virginia. People ran out of their houses to see him. The crowd pressed around his horse. Women begged for locks of his hair. They wanted buttons from his coat and hairs from his horse's tail–anything to prove that they'd really seen him. Tom was embarrassed. He felt that God should get the credit for his success.

His next success came at Harpers Ferry. On September 15, the Union troops surrendered. Tom had hit them with artillery fire from three directions. Again, his men feasted on what they found. Once more Tom could not escape his fame. He had taken thousands of Union prisoners. They wanted a chance to see the famous general before he returned to Maryland.

Lee's plan was for his army to reunite at Sharpsburg, Maryland, near the Antietam Creek. With his army together again, Lee waited for the Union attack. At dawn on September 17, 1862, Union troops started firing. As usual, McClellan had more soldiers than the Confederates. But he didn't use them all at once, and only attacked a little at a time.

At about noon, one of Tom's staff rode up with some peaches. He shared them with the general.

It was the first food that Tom had eaten all day. One myth about Tom was that he was always sucking lemons. Several times during the war, he was seen eating lemons. But he didn't eat them all the time. He liked all kinds of fruit, and peaches were his favorite.

Tom later said that he had never felt so calm in battle as he did on that day at Antietam. He felt that God was protecting him. It's strange that Tom felt so safe. There were over 23,000 casualties that day. Forty percent of Tom's men were killed or wounded. It was the bloodiest day of the Civil War.

If McClellan had kept pounding the Confederates, he could have won a big victory. But he didn't. Under cover of darkness and fog, the Confederates slipped back into Virginia. A few Union soldiers came after them at Shepherdstown. But Tom and his men turned them away.

President Lincoln did two things after the Battle of Antietam or Sharpsburg. He fired McClellan, and he announced the Emancipation Proclamation. It said that slaves would be set free in any state that

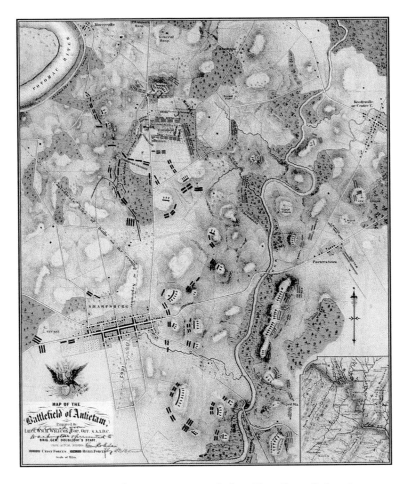

This military map of the Battle of Antietam shows Union forces in red and Confederate troops in blue. In that bloody battle, Tom lost almost half his men.

didn't rejoin the Union by January 1, 1863. The North had been fighting to save the Union. Now it had another goal: to free the slaves.

This illustration shows men playing baseball in a Confederate camp. Because there were often long periods between battles, troops kept themselves occupied while in camp.

6

The Final Battles

After the Battle of Antietam, Tom and his troops spent several fairly quiet months in the Shenandoah Valley. People sent him all kinds of gifts—cakes, chairs, and saddles. But his men were in need of more basic things. He told Anna to pull up all the carpets. His men needed them for blankets.

In October 1862, Tom was promoted to lieutenant general. Lee put him in charge of half of the Army of Northern Virginia. Tom didn't look much like a general. His clothes were often wrinkled and dust-covered and he wore an old hat.

Another general sent him a jacket trimmed with

gold lace. Jackson tried it on, just to be polite. Then he packed it away. In his letter to Anna, he said he liked simple things.

While Tom was back in the valley, the war began to heat up to the east. General Ambrose Burnside was now in charge of the Union army in Virginia. Burnside wanted to gain control of the hills around Fredericksburg. But he needed special floating bridges to move his troops across the Rappahannock River. The bridges arrived late. In the meantime, the Confederates took over the hills. Lee ordered Tom east.

While Tom was marching to Fredericksburg, he learned that Anna had given birth to a baby girl on November 23. Jackson named her Julia Laura, after his mother and sister.

The Battle of Fredericksburg took place on December 13. While Tom and his men defended a wooded area, the main action took place on Marye's Heights. Burnside sent wave after wave of men up the hill. With more than 12,000 casualties, it was a total disaster for the Union.

In January 1863, Burnside tried to attack the Confederates again. But his troops got bogged down in mud. He was soon replaced by General Joseph Hooker. The armies of the North and the South spent the winter looking at each other across the river. Tom used the time to write battle reports. He also worked on getting more **chaplains**. Tom respected all religions. He didn't care which church the chaplains came from. He just wanted his men to have religious services.

Tom longed to see Anna and the baby. In mid-April, Anna set off with five-month-old Julia and a nurse. They arrived on a rainy Monday. Tom met the train. "When he entered the coach to receive us," Anna said, "his rubber overcoat was dripping from the rain which was falling, but his face was all sunshine and gladness."

The family had nine happy days together in a house near Tom's headquarters. But that all ended early on the morning of April 29. Hooker's army was on the move. Tom told Anna to pack up and go home. Then he hurried away. As soon as he

Tom (standing, left) leads his men in prayer. Belief in God was important to Tom, who wanted his men to attend religious services.

left, cannons began firing. The house shook and windows rattled.

The attack was part of a trick. Hooker had already taken much of his army away. Now he planned to surprise Lee by attacking from behind. Lee soon discovered what Hooker was up to. Hooker had twice as many men as Lee did. But Lee still decided to divide his army. He left some troops at Fredericksburg, while he and Tom took the rest of the army to meet Hooker at Chancellorsville.

Hooker decided to wait for Lee to attack. On May 1, Lee and Tom met to make plans. Lee divided his army once more. He would stay to face Hooker. Meanwhile Tom would take 28,000 men on a 12-mile march to get around Hooker's men and surprise them.

On the morning of May 2, they started marching. Union troops caught sight of them, but they thought the Confederates were retreating. By late afternoon, Tom's men were in position. Union troops were busy cooking dinner. Suddenly the Confederates burst from the woods and the Union troops ran off in confusion.

Around nine o'clock that night, Tom and a few men rode out to check what was going on. Somehow they got in front of their own battle line. The Confederates thought that Jackson and his men were Union soldiers, so they started firing. Tom was hit once in the right hand, and twice in the left arm. He was almost knocked to the ground and his horse ran away. A stretcher arrived to take him to safety but Union soldiers started to fire at Tom and his men. One of the men carrying the stretcher fell. Tom tumbled to the ground. Someone held him down to keep him from being killed. They finally made it to a horse-drawn ambulance. It bumped down the road to a field hospital. Tom's left arm was broken and would have to be amputated. A doctor removed the arm two inches below the shoulder.

At first, it seemed that Tom would recover. Hours after his operation, he was awake and giving orders. But by May 7, he was having trouble breathing. Pneumonia had set in. Anna and Julia arrived that day.

By Sunday, May 10, Tom's doctor knew the general had only a few hours to live. "I have always desired to die on Sunday," Tom said. In his last few moments, he seemed to think he was on a battlefield. He gave orders to one of his generals. Then he said, "Let us cross over the river and rest under the shade of the trees."

This illustration shows Tom as he is wounded in both the hand and arm. Although it seemed that he would recover, Tom died eight days after he was wounded.

Tom was 39 years old when he died. His body was taken to Richmond. All businesses were closed. The streets were filled with mourners. Tom was buried in Lexington, Virginia.

At the end of May, the First Virginia Brigade

officially became the Stonewall Brigade. Tom had always said that the name Stonewall belonged to his men and not to himself.

The South was stunned by Tom's death. Lee never found anyone who could replace him. Tom was an expert at moving his troops quickly and secretly. He often attacked from the side or from behind. Without Tom, Lee stopped using this type of attack. At the Battle of Gettysburg in July 1863, Lee attacked head-on. The result was a terrible loss for the South.

Lee later said that if Tom had lived, the South would have won at Gettysburg. And then, he believed, the South would have won the war.

Instead, the war went on for another two years. The South finally surrendered in the spring of 1865. Would the results have been different if Stonewall Jackson had lived? No one knows. But that question is still asked today.

GLOSSARY

arsenal–a place where guns and ammunition are made or kept

artillery–large guns, such as cannons

baptize–to pour water on a person's head or dip that person in water to show that he or she is now a Christian

casualties–soldiers killed, wounded, or missing in battle

chaplain–a minister, priest, or rabbi who serves in the military

constable–a public officer responsible for keeping the peace

deacon–a person who helps with the pastor's work

debts–money owed to another person

desert–to leave without permission

hydropathy–drinking and bathing in water from natural springs for medical reasons

military campaign–a grand plan for a series of battles

pastor–a minister or clergyman

retreat–to move away from a battle

secede–to withdraw from an organization

troops–soldiers

truce–a time when both sides in a battle agree not to fight

volunteers–people who do something because they want to, not because they have to do it

CHRONOLOGY ════════════════════

1824   Born Thomas J. Jackson on January 21 in Clarksburg, Virginia (now West Virginia).

1846   Graduates from West Point.

1846–48   Serves with the U.S. army in the Mexican War.

1849–51   Serves with the army at Fort Hamilton, New York, and Fort Meade, Florida; becomes a professor at Virginia Military Institute in Lexington, Virginia.

1853   Marries Elinor Junkin on August 4.

1854   Elinor Junkin Jackson delivers stillborn son on October 22 and dies.

1857   Marries Mary Anna Morrison on July 16.

1858   Daughter, Mary Graham, is born on April 30 and dies on May 25.

1861   Leaves Lexington for the Civil War in April; promoted to brigadier general in July; fights in the First Battle of Manassas in July; gets his "Stonewall" nickname.

1862   Leads his famous Valley campaign in spring; fights in Seven Days campaign in June; fights at the Second Battle of Manassas in July; fights the Battle of Antietam in September; promoted to lieutenant general in October; daughter, Julia Laura, is born on November 23; fights at Fredericksburg in December.

1863   Accidentally shot by his own men at Chancellorsville on May 2; dies on May 10.

CIVIL WAR TIME LINE ═══════════

1860   Abraham Lincoln is elected president of the United States on November 6. During the next few months, Southern states begin to break away from the Union.

1861   On April 12, the Confederates attack Fort Sumter, South Carolina, and the Civil War begins. Union forces are defeated in Virginia at the First Battle of Bull Run (First Manassas) on July 21 and withdraw to Washington, D.C.

1862   Robert E. Lee is placed in command of the main Confederate army in Virginia in June. Lee defeats the Army of the Potomac at the Second Battle of Bull Run (Second Manassas) in Virginia on August 29–30. On September 17, Union general George B. McClellan turns back Lee's first invasion of the North at Antietam Creek near Sharpsburg, Maryland. It is the bloodiest day of the war.

1863   On January 1, President Lincoln issues the Emancipation Proclamation, freeing slaves in Southern states. Between May 1–6, Lee wins an important victory at Chancellorsville, but key Southern commander Thomas J. "Stonewall" Jackson dies from wounds. In June, Union forces hold the city of Vicksburg, Mississippi, under siege. The people of Vicksburg surrender on July 4. Lee's second invasion of the North during July 1–3 is decisively turned back at Gettysburg, Pennsylvania.

1864 General Grant is made supreme Union commander on March 9. Following a series of costly battles, on June 19 Grant successfully encircles Lee's troops in Petersburg, Virginia. A siege of the town lasts nearly a year. Union general William Sherman captures Atlanta on September 2 and begins the "March to the Sea," a campaign of destruction across Georgia and South Carolina. On November 8, Abraham Lincoln wins reelection as president.

1865 On April 2, Petersburg, Virginia, falls to the Union. Lee attempts to reach Confederate forces in North Carolina but is gradually surrounded by Union troops. Lee surrenders to Grant on April 9 at Appomattox, Virginia, ending the war. Abraham Lincoln is assassinated by John Wilkes Booth on April 14.

FURTHER READING

Brewer, Paul. *The American Civil War*. Austin, Tex.: Raintree Steck-Vaughn, 1999.

Grabowski, Patricia A. *Robert E. Lee*. Philadelphia: Chelsea House Publishers, 2001.

Green, Carl R. and William R. Sanford. *Confederate Generals of the Civil War*. Springfield, N.J.: Enslow Publishers, 1998.

Hakim, Joy. *War, Terrible War*. New York: Oxford University Press, 1994.

Robertson, James I., Jr. *Civil War! America Becomes One Nation*. New York: Alfred A. Knopf, 1996.

Smith, Carter. *The First Battles: A Sourcebook on the Civil War*. Brookfield, Conn.: The Millbrook Press, 1993.

INDEX

PICTURE CREDITS

page

3: The Library of Congress
6: New Millennium Images
11: New Millennium Images
14: National Archives
18: The Library of Congress
21: The Library of Congress
25: New Millennium Images
28: The Library of Congress
30: The Library of Congress
34: The Library of Congress
39: New York Public Library/
    Picture Collections

42: The Library of Congress
47: The Library of Congress
49: National Archives
54: The Library of Congress
59: The Library of Congress
63: The Library of Congress
64: The Library of Congress
68: New York Public Library/
    Picture Collections
71: The Library of Congress

ABOUT THE AUTHOR

MARTHA S. HEWSON is a freelance writer and editor who works on projects for children and adults. She is a former editor at the *Philadelphia Inquirer* and *McCall's* magazine. She has a bachelor's degree in American history and literature from Harvard and a master's degree in journalism from Columbia. She lives near Philadelphia.

Senior Consulting Editor **ARTHUR M. SCHLESINGER, JR.** is the leading American historian of our time. He won the Pulitzer Prize for his book *The Age of Jackson* (1945), and again for *A Thousand Days* (1965). This chronicle of the Kennedy Administration also won a National Book Award. He has written many other books, including a multi-volume series, *The Age of Roosevelt.* Professor Schlesinger is the Albert Schweitzer Professor of the Humanities at the City University of New York, and has been involved in several other Chelsea House projects, including the COLONIAL LEADERS series of biographies on the most prominent figures of early American history.